**Dedicated to our husbands,
Morgan and Bud**

Lemon Why Are You Yellow?
Text copyright © 2019 by Shelby Torgersen
Illustrations copyright © 2019 by Ashlee Waters
All rights reserved. No part of this book may be used or
reproduced in any manner whatsoever without written
permission given by the author except in the case of brief
quotations embodied in critical articles or reviews.
Thank you for purchasing a copy of this book and for complying
with copyright laws.
Published by Cuddly Cloud Books.
For questions or for further information please visit cuddlycloudbooks.com

Written by Shelby Torgersen
Illustrated by Ashlee Waters

ISBN: 978-1-7341246-0-6 (hardcover)
978-1-7341246-1-3 (ebook)
Library of Congress Control Number: 2019915602

Printed in PRC
First addition: 2019
10 9 8 7 6 5 4 3 2 1

LEMON
Why Are You Yellow?

written by Shelby Torgersen
illustrated by Ashlee Waters

Today my friend asked me
a really big question.

"Lemon, why are you yellow?" she said. I thought really hard, and scratched my yellow head.

Ah-ha! I think I know why I'm yellow, I do! It's the same reason that my friend Blueberry is blue.

You see, my mom's yellow, my dad's yellow, and my grandpa is too!
My grandma is actually kind of green, you can see that in my hue.

My yellow actually started many, many years ago. My great-great-great-grandpa Huey told me so!

He started as a seed, and he grew our family tree! You see that's why I'm yellow, it was passed from him to me.

You see, my mom's yellow, my dad's yellow, and my grandpa is too! My grandma is actually kind of green, you can see that in my hue.

Ah-ha! I think I know why I'm yellow, I do! It's the same reason that my friend Blueberry is blue.

"Lemon, why are you yellow?" she said. I thought really hard, and scratched my yellow head.

Today my friend asked me a really big question.

LEMON
Why Are You Yellow?

written by Shelby Torgersen
illustrated by Ashlee Waters

The yellow was passed down from lemon to lemon. I guess the first lemons got their yellows from heaven.

This is my friend Banana, and he is yellow too! But my skin's kinda bumpy, while his is nice and smooth.

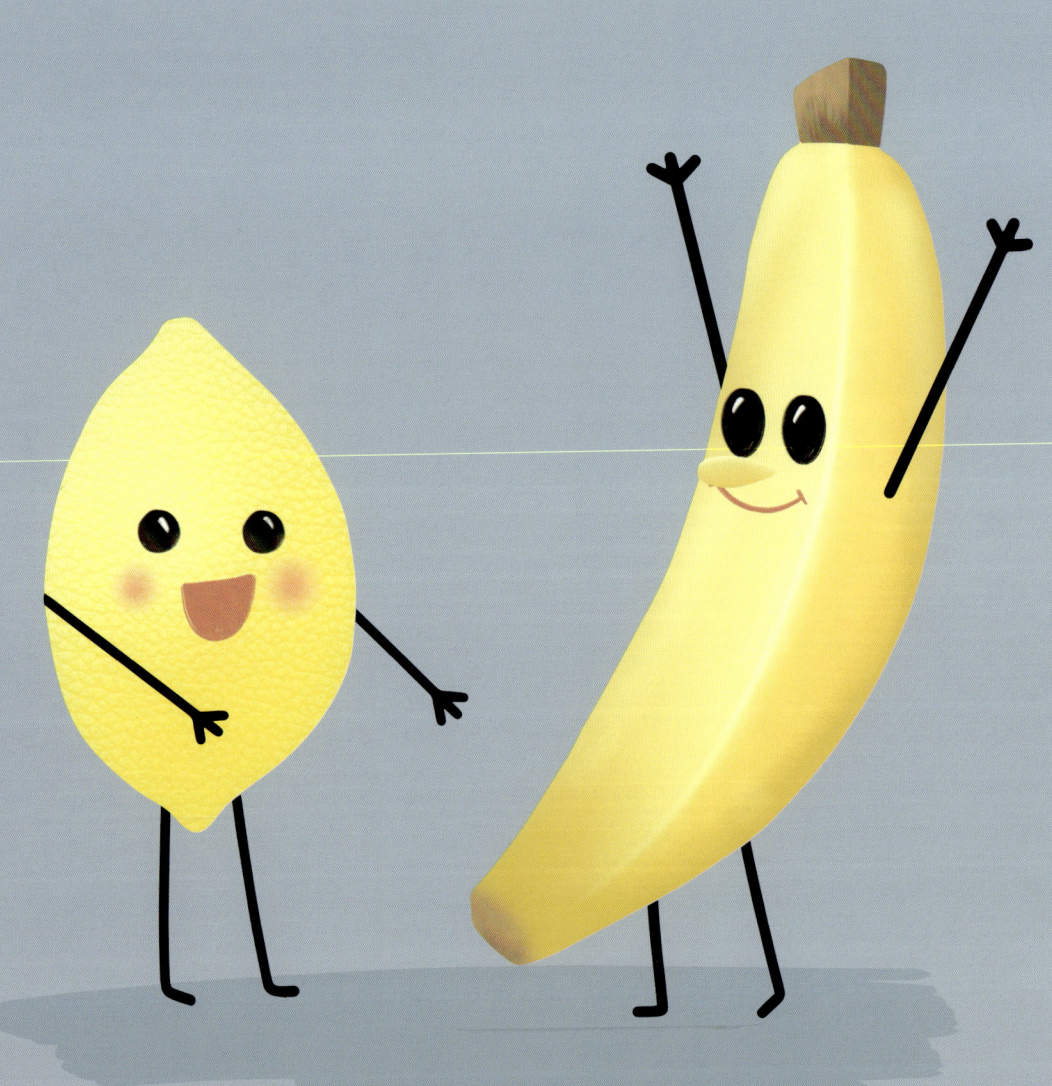

Every fruit is different, our skins are different shades. We get it from our family and that is how it's made.

So yes we all are different,
but all of us are cute.

I think we're best together.
They call it "mixed fruit!"